D1088825

WHERE DO THEY GO? INSECTS IN WINTER

WHERE DO THEY GO? INSECTS IN WINTER

BY MILLICENT E. SELSAM
ILLUSTRATED BY ARABELLE WHEATLEY

FOUR WINDS PRESS • NEW YORK

For Robert and Priscilla and Margaret

LIBRARY OF CONGRESS CATALOGING IN PUBLICATION DATA

Selsam, Millicent Ellis, 1912–
    Where do they go? Insects in Winter

Summary: Explains how some insects fly south for the winter and others spend the
cold months underground, underwater, in unused buildings, or as eggs or pupae.
1. Insects—Wintering—Juvenile literature.   [1. Insects—Habits and behavior. 2. Winter] I. Title.
QL496.S4   595.7′054′3   82-70976   ISBN 0-590-07862-3   AACR2

Published by Four Winds Press. A Division of Scholastic Inc., New York, N.Y.
Copyright © 1982 by Millicent E. Selsam. All rights reserved. Printed in the United States of America.
Library of Congress Catalog Card Number: 82-70976
1 2 3 4 5 86 85 84 83 82

Contents

Winter comes

In spring, summer, and fall, insects are everywhere.
Bumblebees buzz.
Flies and dragonflies zoom around.
Caterpillars munch on leaves.
Mosquitoes bite people and suck plant juices.
Crickets and katydids sing.
Butterflies and moths unfold their wings and fly.

Then winter comes.
Snow and ice cover the ground and the branches of trees.
Ponds and lakes freeze over.
The insects disappear.
Where do they go?

Where are the pesky flies and mosquitoes?

Adult houseflies and mosquitoes find places in barns, attics, cellars, and unused bedrooms and spend the winter there. Outside they may stay in caves, or holes in tree trunks — any place that offers a little protection from the cold.

Most of them are females that mated during the summer. The eggs they carry inside them can develop into more flies and mosquitoes when spring comes.

If you look around in a country house that has been kept cool all winter, you will find lots and lots of flies. Many of them look dead. Many of them really are dead. But if you warm up the house, some of the flies warm up and start buzzing around.

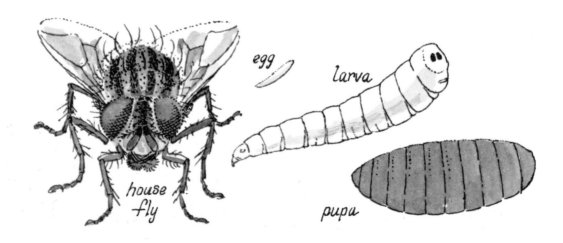

egg

larva

house fly

pupa

Each female fly that lives through the winter can lay a hundred eggs at a time. These eggs may hatch within twenty-four hours. They turn into adult flies in two weeks.

The female fly can live for two more months, and during that time she can lay about five batches of eggs. So it pays to swat each fly you see.

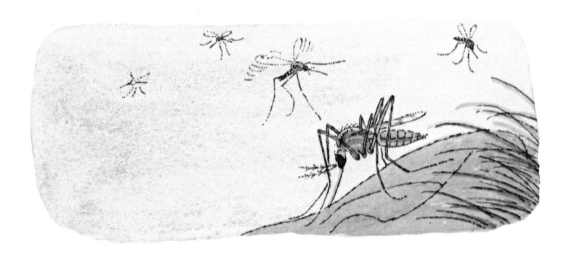

In the spring, each female mosquito that lives through the winter lays her eggs. She may die soon after. But the eggs are laid in little puddles or pools of water where the young stages of mosquitoes can develop.

Soon there are lots more mosquitoes.

Where are the beetles and bugs?

Potato beetles, ground beetles, and cucumber beetles dig down into the ground where it is warmer.

Wood-boring beetles crawl into deep holes or cracks in the bark of trees. They stay there, barely alive, until spring.

Thousands of ladybird beetles pile up one on top of the other in tree stumps or under rocks and leaves and lie there all winter. Sometimes, on a warm day, they may move around a little.

In California, ladybird beetles fly high up in the mountains in the fall. Millions of them spend the winter there among the dead leaves and branches of the forest floor. People go there to gather them and load them onto trucks. Then they sell the beetles to farmers who use them to fight many plant pests.

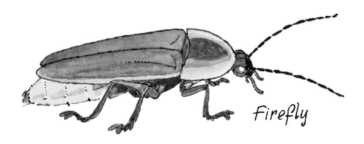

Firefly

Some beetles, such as fireflies (did you know they are beetles?), hatch out of their eggs at the end of the summer. They spend the winter in a young stage called a *larva* (**lahr**-vuh). The *larvae* (**lahr**-vee) look like short worms. They do what adult beetles do in the winter. They tunnel down into the ground. It is warmer there.

Many bugs spend the winter in the same way as beetles. Adult squash bugs and lace bugs hide under leaves, weeds, stones, or bark. Flat bark bugs hide in cracks and holes in trees. Burrowing bugs dig down into the earth.

Some bugs hatch out of their eggs in late summer. When they hatch out they are *nymphs*. (This is the name for the young stage of a bug.) The nymphs dig down into the ground until spring.

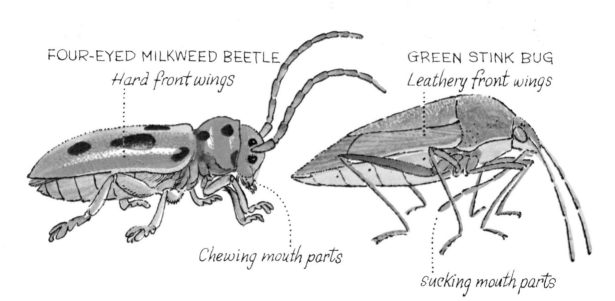

FOUR-EYED MILKWEED BEETLE
Hard front wings

GREEN STINK BUG
Leathery front wings

Chewing mouth parts

sucking mouth parts

Bugs and beetles are both insects. How can you tell a bug from a beetle? Beetles have hard front wings and mouthparts for chewing.

Bugs have soft, leathery front wings and mouthparts for sucking.

What happens to grasshoppers, crickets, and katydids?

In the fall, a female grasshopper drills deep holes in the soft earth. She lays from twenty to a hundred eggs. Then she dies, but the eggs last through the winter.

In the spring the eggs hatch into tiny grasshoppers. They look like their parents, but they are much smaller and do not have wings. They are called nymphs. A nymph molts (sheds its skin) five to eight times as it grows. It takes several months to grow wings and become an adult grasshopper.

The female cricket also lays eggs in the earth and dies soon after. She lays a few hundred eggs. Each egg is in a separate hole. Young cricket nymphs hatch from the eggs in the spring.

On summer nights we hear katydids snapping *katy-did*, *katy-didn't*. As the evenings grow chilly, the katydids make a shorter, lower sound. Then it gets cold, and the katydids no longer sing. Soon they will die. But the female katydid has laid rows of eggs in the slits of branches or on the edges of leaves. New young katydid nymphs will come out of those eggs in the spring.

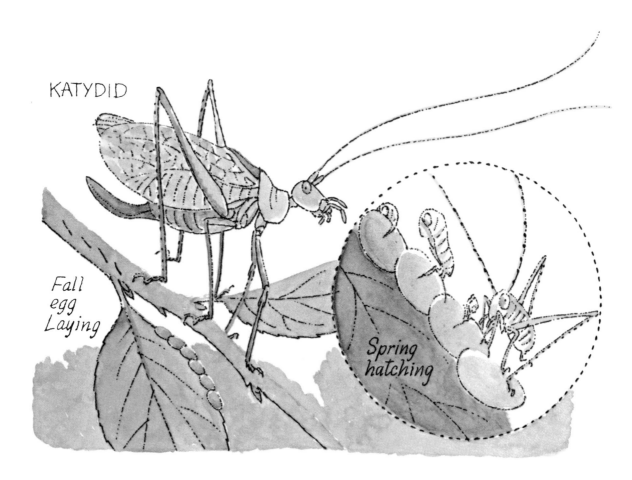

KATYDID

Fall
egg
Laying

Spring
hatching

The praying mantis also dies and leaves eggs that hatch in the spring. In late summer, the female squeezes out a liquid that looks like the foam of a bubble bath. She lays her eggs inside the foam. The foam hardens into a tough case. In the spring, tiny mantises hatch out. They, too, are nymphs. They shed their skin seven times as they grow bigger.

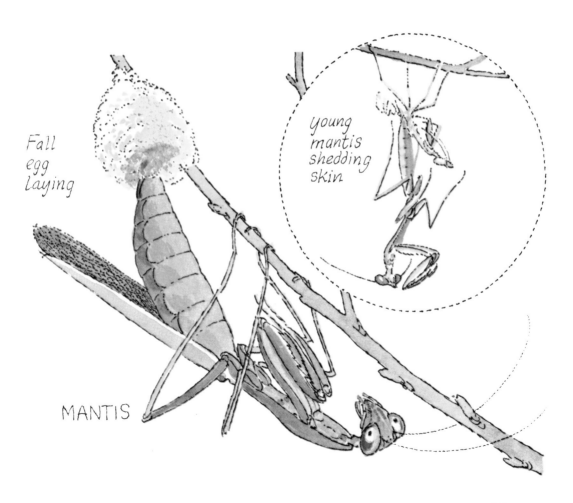

Fall egg laying

young mantis shedding skin

MANTIS

Where are the bees and ants?

Ants have hideaways in the earth all year round. But when winter comes, they crawl down deeper to where the ground does not freeze. There they huddle together to keep warm.

When winter comes, the honeybee queen and the worker bees pile up into a ball in the center of the hive. The bees in the center are warm. The bees on the outside are cold, so they push their way into the middle of the ball. The bees who were in the middle are pushed toward the outside of the ball. Because of this, the ball of bees keeps moving a little bit all the time.

If it gets very, very cold, all the bees move closer, and the ball gets tighter. But the pushing in toward the center keeps on.

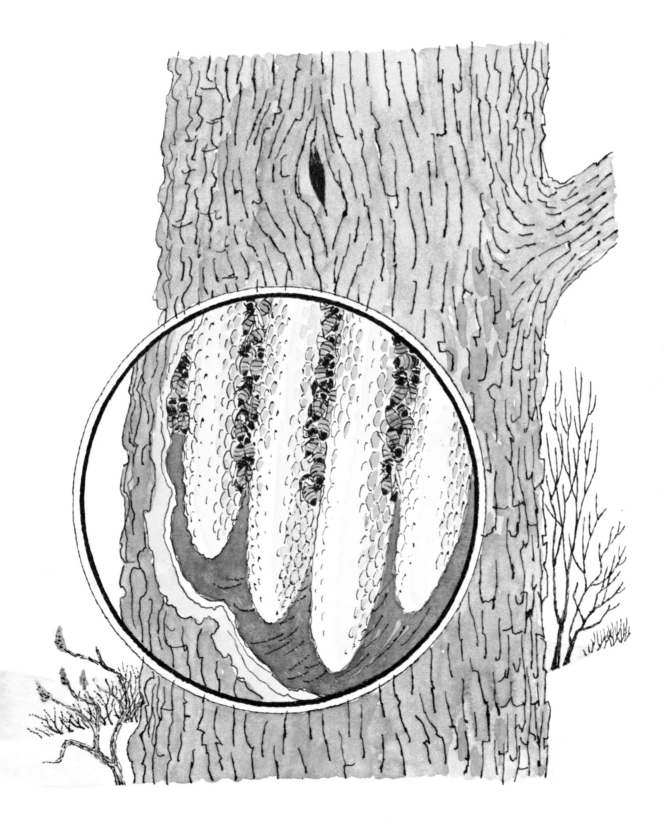

Young bumblebee queens are the only members of the
bumblebee colony that live through the winter. In the
fall, all the other members of the colony lie stiff and
cold. They are dead. But each queen finds a place at the
bottom of a hole in a tree. Or she may dig a hole in the
ground. She might even use an old mouse hole or an
empty mole hole. The hole has to be deep enough so
that she will not freeze.

The bumblebee queen stays in her nest all winter. In the spring, she builds a cup of soft brown wax inside the nest. She gathers pollen and nectar and puts them in the cup. The cup is about the size of a grape. The bumblebee queen lays about ten eggs inside the cup and seals it with wax. Twenty-two days later, the young bumblebees fly out of the nest.

Where are the butterflies?

Early in the spring, even before the leaves of the trees unfold, you can see the mourning cloak fluttering through the bare branches of the woods.

The mourning cloak butterfly has purple wings with gold borders. Just inside the gold border is a row of blue spots. All winter the mourning cloak butterfly rests in a hole in the trunk or branch of an elm or willow tree. Its wings are closed. It looks like a dead leaf because the undersides of its wings are brown.

The monarch butterfly does not stay through the winter like the mourning cloak. Instead, it flies south like the birds.

All summer monarch butterflies sip nectar from milkweed flowers. In August you can see them gathering together. They are getting ready to fly south. Each butterfly weighs about as much as two rose petals. Yet it can fly more than two thousand miles!

After their long trip, the monarchs rest all winter in cool spots in California and Central Mexico. In early spring, the days begin to grow longer. The air gets warmer. The monarchs begin to move their wings. Then they mate and start the long journey back.

Most of the males die on the way. But the females stop and lay eggs on milkweed plants. The eggs hatch, and in about three weeks new butterflies are flying back with the older ones that came from Mexico.

Inside this chrysalis,
the insect is changing into
a black swallowtail butterfly.
In the spring a black-and-yellow
butterfly with "tails" on its hind wings
will come out of the chrysalis.

Where are all the other butterflies?

If you know what a rabbit looks like, you can recognize it whether it is young or old. It just gets bigger as it grows. But many insects change a lot as they grow. You may be seeing butterflies all winter without knowing it. A young butterfly does not look at all like an adult butterfly.

Every butterfly starts out as an egg and some butterflies stay in the egg stage all winter.

But then the butterfly eggs hatch out into caterpillars. Caterpillars munch leaves all summer long. But what happens to a caterpillar in winter?

Although you can find some butterfly eggs and caterpillars in the winter, most butterfly caterpillars change into something else before winter comes. They become *pupae* (**pyoo**-pee). A pupa is a stage in the growth of an insect when it changes from a larva (a caterpillar is a larva) to an adult. A butterfly pupa is also called a *chrysalis* (**criss**-a-liss).

If you go butterfly-hunting in the winter, look for eggs; look for caterpillars rolled up in leaves; look for pupae. And look for adult butterflies, too. You may find one.

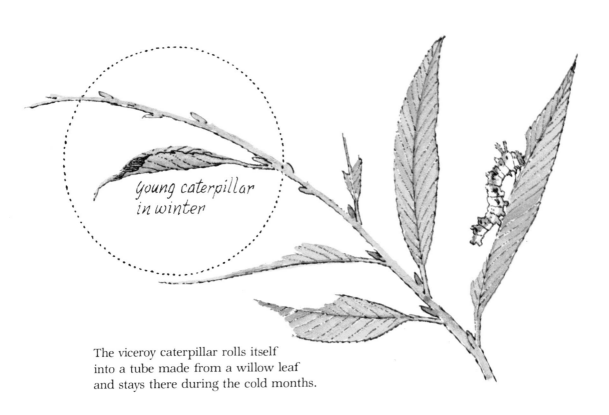

young caterpillar in winter

The viceroy caterpillar rolls itself into a tube made from a willow leaf and stays there during the cold months.

Spicebush
silk moth
cocoon

Where are the moths?

Like the butterflies, moths change as they grow. They also spend the winter as eggs, caterpillars, and pupae. The pupa of a moth is inside a silky overcoat called a *cocoon*. Most moths spend the winter inside their cocoons.

Many cocoons are hard to find in the winter because they are brown or gray and often fall to the floor of the forest. Other cocoons are easier to find because they stay attached to the thin branches to which they are fastened.

luna moth
cocoon

Where are the water insects?

There are almost one million kinds of insects, but only a few thousand live in the water or on it.

When it gets cold, and ice forms on ponds and lakes, many beetles and bugs burrow into the soft mud at the bottom.

Dragonflies, damselflies, and mayflies may spend the winter as eggs stuck in the mud under the water. Or they spend the winter underwater in the nymph stage. In this stage they do not look like the adults at all. They have no wings. They crawl around the bottom eating other insects until it gets so cold that they stop moving and lie quietly in the mud.

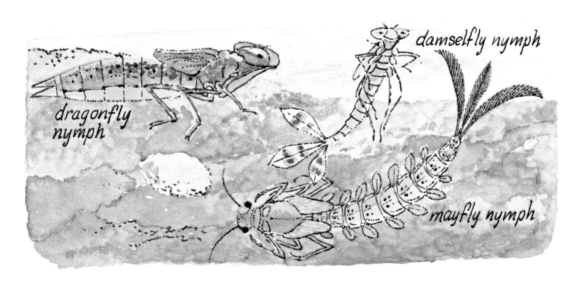

dragonfly nymph

damselfly nymph

mayfly nymph

When spring comes the nymphs climb up plant stems, cast off their skins, and fly into the air on their delicate wings.

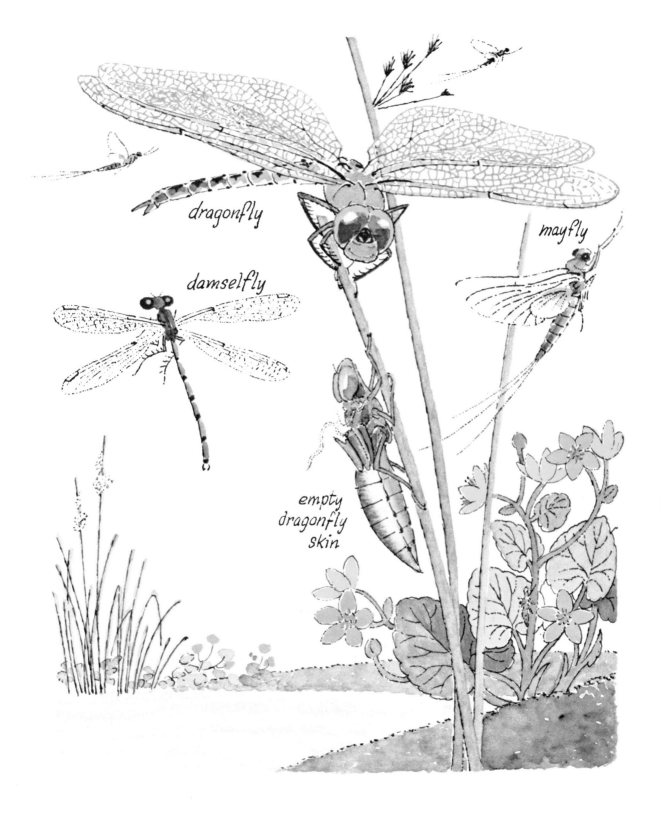

dragonfly

mayfly

damselfly

empty
dragonfly
skin

On a warm day in spring

The winter is cold. The ground is frozen.
The trees are bare. But hidden away there are:
   grasshopper and cricket eggs in the ground,
   honeybees clustered together in their hives,
   mosquito eggs in tree holes or hollows in the soil,
   dragonfly eggs in the mud at the bottom of a pond,
   cocoons swinging from the trees,
   bumblebee queens in old mouse holes.

On a warm day in spring
  the eggs will hatch,
  the bee colonies will stir,
  bugs and beetles will warm up and start to
    move around,
  butterflies and moths will come
    out of their pupa cases and cocoons,
and insects will again zoom and buzz and munch and
fly and do everything that insects do in the summertime.

A Note from the Author

On page 22 you read that a monarch butterfly weighs about as much as two rose petals. Well, there is a story behind this.

I first wrote that a monarch butterfly weighs only *one-fiftieth of an ounce*. My editor said, "Who knows what one-fiftieth of an ounce is? Can you find something—maybe a grain of popcorn—that weighs exactly the same as the butterfly?"

It was easy to get the popcorn, and I happened to have a balance scale that could weigh tiny, tiny amounts. The scale was so delicate that it moved when you breathed on it. But where would I find a monarch butterfly in the wintertime? That same week, at a party, I met a friend who had a dried monarch butterfly. She said I could have it!

I put the butterfly on one side of the balance scale. Then I put a small piece of popcorn on the other side. Too heavy! The scale tipped all the way down on the popcorn side.

What else could I try? I looked around. I had a rose in a vase on my desk. Would two rose petals weigh the same as a two-winged butterfly? I weighed them, but the petals were too heavy.

I thought, *the butterfly is dry. The petals are fresh and moist. I must let the petals dry, too.* I let the rose petals dry overnight. In the morning I tried again. The rose petals and the butterfly weighed exactly the same!

Now I know that a monarch butterfly (dried) weighs as much as two rose petals (dried).